I0756306

FINISHING LINE PRESS
www.finishinglinepress.com

guilty as an orchid

sonnets and poems by

richard haney-jardine

Finishing Line Press
Georgetown, Kentucky

guilty as an orchid

Dedicated to Tony Greisinger,
most generous supporter and sympathetic reader.

"Cuando yo muero quiero tus manos en mis ojos:
quiero la luz y el trigo de tus manos amadas
pasar una vez más sobre mí su frescura:
sentir la suavidad que cambió mis destino."

—"Soneta de la noche," Pablo Neruda

ISBN 979-8-89990-475-2 First Edition

ACKNOWLEDGMENTS

With the kind permission of *The Iowa Review*, the following poems from their Winter 2023/2024 issue are reprinted here: "lifesavers" and "jonah and the whale," as well as earlier versions of "lightbulb" and "piss poor."

A substantially different version of "jonah and the whale" appeared earlier in the anthology, *Habits: The Good, The Bad, and The Ugly,* © 2023 reprinted here with the permission of Public Poetry Press.

An earlier version of the poem "dispatches from amnesty international" is reprinted here from the anthology "One Page Poetry," © 2025 with permission of Prometheus Books/*The 2025 One Page Anthology*, Colin Graham, editor.

The author gratefully acknowledges Finishing Line Press for the publication of this chapbook.

Publisher: Leah Huete de Maines
Editor: Christen Kincaid
Cover Art: Anthony Greisinger © 2025
Cover Author Photo: Kathryn Haney © 2023
Interior Author Photo: William Taylor © 2024
Cover Design: Elizabeth Maines McCleavy

Order online: www.finishinglinepress.com
also available on amazon.com

Author inquiries and mail orders:
Finishing Line Press
PO Box 1626
Georgetown, Kentucky 40324
USA

Contents

1. i doubt that day understands night

Just fifteen when I left the sun of home
saw snow for the first time falling on tombs.

It wasn't proof of angels, it was ashes
of grief, a ticker tape parade awash

with silence on a black and white TV
a celebration not of victory

but a defeat, the swift dissolution
of what I might have been, a sudden end.

I doubt that day understands night, that sun
understands moon, that boy understands man

that salt understands sugar, that the tree
understands the bird, snow understood me.

For months I did not glance at my own image
but like Narcissus metamorphosed, changed.

2. thirteen (fourteen) ways of looking at the faggot
(after stevens)

nineteen-eighty-six: 28,712 cases reported
24,599 deaths

i.

rising from the sea
blond mane sequined
with buds of algae
and salt, beautiful
guilty as an orchid

ii.

two razors at the sink
rabid with foam

iii.

a flying dutchman who never
comes to port, a tern exiled
to a vast, unrelenting sea of hope
hope the underling of love
still blossoming

iv.

four long white tube-socks
coiled, spent like condoms
bedside serpents

v.

put to sleep
like an african violet
barely touched
shrunk
into himself

vi.

six republicans at
seven sentinel urinals
jangling coins, pretending
not to watch, pinstriped

vii.

stamens furled in an urgent
flower, a motor on the verge
of turning over, a dam
of stemmed power
a humming motel door
but housekeeping knows

viii.

the eighth-grade math teacher
forever sealed his moustache
behind the chaste kiss of marriage.
he still lingers, after football games.

ix.

it's funny the things he'd forgotten
about his childhood home
the number of chandeliers, for instance.
bouquets of chandeliers.

x.

the eagle phone perched on its cradle
waiting to feast at the first dispatch.
Prometheus has stolen fire
but it's ten, and he hasn't called.

xi.

from the prom he never went to
a corsage at his breast burst
like carmine ink from a pen
blooming into his chest.

xii.

in the struggle of the other's
arms, they lay turbaned in sheets
breastbone against breast-
bone, twelve ribs each
none taken, none broken.

xiii.

wearing just your shirt or mine, we've
ceded more than wardrobe, you
gather me up from my dreams
with a smile that stitches through
the smallest petals of my sleep.
how perilous it seemed at first, two
men in love, dear God, but now
at table, your flesh mortifies me
elbows touching. We. Must. Live. How?

xiv.

Now!

3. lifesavers

Woodstock, Ontario: blue delphinium sky
this side of pitch, summer barreling with us

to a Super 8 Motel. What compares
to those nine cherry Life Savers I guided

like missiles into your mouth until Exit
10 to keep you awake? You in the mirror

towel wrapped tight above your groin, your wrists
thick with pulse, your nipples blooming with hair?

Watching you shave, putting six quarters into
the bedside slot, thinking hard of untying

the knot as that bed jerked me? Or when you
buck naked now, turned towards me, unsuspecting

not knowing it's possible to fall—waiting
not knowing it's possible to fall—waiting
for one damned traffic light to change—in love?

4. lightbulb

Nature is constantly stating the obvious.
I'm a tree, says the elm. I'm just a mountain
says Mount Blue. It doesn't say, *Climb up, then.*
The tree doesn't suggest, *Swing in my branches.*

We'd be better off if we looked at clocks
said, *It's about ten, time for bed,* then dropped
to lift the dog from the rug, climbed upstairs
let sleep come, which wouldn't ask questions, either.

Why wallow in shallow seas of nuances?
Make it simple, *Join me tonight.* Forget
puzzles like, Tomorrow is garbage day
by which you signal, *It's your turn, baby.*

Lightbulb's out, which means, *Change it.* And I'd change
anything for you. Anything but change.

5. icelandic poppy sunrise

i.

Do we insist seas theorize on where their first waves began?
Demand saplings hypothesize why their limbs are so friable?
Interrogate nestlings why they can't soar from birth?

ii.

Some things—goat kids, for instance, can rise to their fore-
and back legs, seconds after delivery, strong though still
slick from the aspic of their mother's amniotic sack.
(We've seen it on TV, from the guardrails of recliners...)
Dolphins, who stain the sea with their placental blood
deliver their calves ripe enough to swim free, solo
in the ocean's laboratory-medium gel, thick with intent.
(We've seen this on TV, perched on our beds...)
And brush turkeys, liberated from shells that smothered them
arise, decked already with sleek, full-flight feathers
and fast as a tear is wiped, can abandon their nests and fly.
(That too, we've seen on TV, from a treadmill...)

iii.

But you and I, we must watch it all—our unfolding as one—not from a TV
but live, in full life, not grilling, not probing, not asking questions.
We must watch the splendor of the wide movie screen of real lives flooding
into the back of our orange retinas, through the membranes that hold back
the lobes of two separate hearts yearning to conjoin.

iv.

Have you considered this? That this advent of us being together as one
might render us unable yet to stand on both legs, make us struggle
from the frailty of beginnings—even if we feel we're already side by side
paw in paw—and need to grow in a slowness of tenderness of helplessness
of the yet unimaginable, the still unknown, and the ever unknowable?

v.

Can you keep this in mind? That this nascent Icelandic poppy sunrise
of our silent, wide-opened gazes—unfussy, persistent, wild, and delicate—
doesn't mean we'll need to speed through intersections, or instead
heed flashing blue or yellow lights, or plead for directions to steer us right
that we will board a ship that's as small as an opened fist and still sail?

vi.

Will you trust me on this? That there will be time for us
to learn that our immigrant love might empty the register of our days
and that though no one has the power to deplete the wealth of the hours
divide them into the small jangling coins of morning, noon, and night
that I'd spend them all—all of the hours—on you?

6. the yolks of your fingertips

i.

They told them, *Don't listen.* Not even the sky's blue.
They put ears to grass in its salad days. Ate green dew.

ii.

What was wrong with love's thumbprint clues? Their whorls?
Were their hands no longer handsome for work still to unfurl?

iii.

They pressed them, *Don't look.* They listened to grasshoppers
flicking blade to blade of grass, nails flying from clippers.

iv.

Spring was a codicil to winter's last testament, then summer's
lightning bugs overwhelmed with light skies laden with stars.
The only remedy was laying their heads down, unremarked
but safe as skulls still slick with skin beneath abundant hair.

v.

They insisted, *Don't taste.* Banned roses from feeding the air
their musk tantalizing, petal-flesh, pluck-ripe, but pinker.

vi.

Everyone's allergic, talks the small on lawns, swats flies.
Caterpillars telegraph on their arms: No Death Only Life.

vii.

They said, *Don't touch.* Postage stamps met their tongues
suns to bared backs, clouds to judgment, trees to lungs.

viii.

Twigs were sturdy enough for palm-sized birds' nests
and making teepees for their campfires in the pretense
there was wilderness in the breastbones of heart-poor chests.

ix.

They demanded, *Don't smell.* But it could not be done.
They demanded too much. To not smell the decaying stone
fruits? Blood's copper penny taste, smelling like nothing
nothing at all? The scent of flies spun in spider lace clothing?
Impossible to smell, not to smell. Scents born to die alone.

x.

The corn had shortened amid dark-winged summer flies.
It was a season for storm. Clouds mothering Earth and Sky.
Rooks profiting from brittle branches, roosting absently.
The sun fulminating poppies. Land buckling, dried Mississippi
mud flat: a time for dark covenant, for torrid-flower sleep.

xi.

Not to listen, look, taste, touch, smell. To embrace deceit.
Glorious world they can't be kept from! A kestrel extended
its wings, flight stupid with smell, like a cross suspended
till sound died and touch's taste couldn't wait one more beat.

xii.

What shall this be called? Hope that yoking two beasts
to plough earth into ruts will help indentured crops be
sellable, feed them? Lust for answering questions that land
on their crowns, niggling? Ants creeping up IV-ready hands?

xiii.

In Spanish "fingertips" is las yemas de los dedos. Fingertips'
yolks, a hint of fledglings' unfolding to flutter into ether
to speak their lips, that time a chick smashes what kept it
from eating sky, egg's shell, bird's suit never grazing ever.

xiv.

I will always want to feel the yolks of your fingertips
hear them, smell, touch, taste, see them, deliver this kiss
even as they turn yellow as the sun's yellow. I want this all
now and in the fall of falls. In our fall. For we will fall.

7. the susan anne

8:45 PM New London to Orient
the full-mooned ferry glides, silently.
I wish it rocked me, would spin
me, would leave me dizzy, make me wobbly:

Such peace on such a night, after
flourishes of operatic guff
flurries of accusations, reminders
that life kills time, is tough

enough without our meddling, slicing
everything as if it were just that one loaf
and not a multitude, as if moons rising
or seas, tied as they are, tied us both.

Tonight, cloud breezes are wisps of hair
on an old lady's head, white, translucent
finally, in half-light, once again, downy, fair
and the hint of fall hasn't betrayed us yet

though it is late August, the peaches
almost over, and our heirloom tomatoes pine
round as the moon that keeps staring at us
orotund, beautiful red vowels on the vine.

8. the herons of spy pond

If the soul is a bird, and the soul lies
in the heart, this slim chest must nest a bird

with wings as vast as the white snowy winter
herons'. Who would dare deny that the flight

of birds is a miracle. We were once
spun inside like angels, significant

as chrysalides and vowed to spend these months
our final days as one, treading the land

silently, watching herons lifting up
from Spy Pond, water from their wings made powder

never waking as they rose to the top
beyond our abilities to see where

two souls might go unfastened from their bones
or if we'd fly together or alone.

9. skinny trees

I want words like gossamer, exquisite
clotheslines in high summer, taut with wood pins

flagging white sheets that flap like angel's wings
his viscous pollen in my mouth, that white

of him. I want dandelions fluffing off
the fields into the sky, diasporas

of them, the tumble of anaphora
from sermons that say, *Let's fuck*. I want troughs

for new fodder. I want the sea the sea
was before we stumbled through skinny trees.

I want limelight hydrangeas, blank nights
that seem sufficient as the day's dark light.

I want Shakespeare, the Bible, and the real
Good Book, the dictionary—cold with zeal.

10. en el autobus (on the city bus)

"les larmes qu'on ne pleure pas…
martèlent le cœur triste et las"
—Blau, Milliet, Harmann, lyricists for Jules Massenet's opera Werther

Do you recall that aria
"Tears we have not wept…
hammer into us"?
I am both the nail and the hammer.
I am both the wall and the floor.
I am heads, and I am tails.

(Me reparo a la alcoba
donde quedó el pie
descalzo de la niñez.
¿Cómo sería morir
en la misma cama
donde nacimos?)

I don't fit into the minuscule
of your infinitude any longer
and I never asked for much…
Just love me, oh, quicksand!
Oh, wrinkled moon, breastfeed me!
I ask for so little and accept nothing.

(Cuando el tiempo se levanta
de buena hora
se queda—como tú—callado.
Ve cómo se montan por sí mismos
los peldaños y quedan sin hablar
cansados de subir y bajar.)

I took the bus to buy some sugar
and oh! that pain I so lacked
and the wake God leaves behind.
No one followed me.
not the secretive wind
nor that singular mouth.

(Las horas que nos robamos
cuentas que nos cuentan
deseos que mueren en el alma
amores que nos fugan
viven en calles sin salidas.)

11. sauna

I inhale, then hold my breath, and I'm eating air
a gesture that reminds me of our love, aspiring
the vanillin of striated irises
deep into our diaphragms as they were expiring.
Alone now, eucalyptus floods my sinuses
as I grasp my toes in a sauna dank with strangers
pretending hard I'm not in fact looking at their junk
waiting to exhale so long, I almost faint. *Fuck.*

Keep it all in the breath, the flowers seemed to say.
Does the real fruit lie in intense inhalation
of things, not also in the languid exhalation
of their aromas? Is it brave to spread the chest
open the larynx to take in muscular breaths?
Gutless to let your scent go, give my breath away?

12. jonah and the whale

The first time he comes home with the big bucks
for giving a massage, his lungs may burst
in fists of laughter in the full bloom of drunk.

He tells himself it's sacred to lay men
upon a table, find that one spot, then
dig into their traps with his stubbled chin.

Starts it legit: Swedish, deep tissue strokes
sneaks in lomi-lomi, then tantra, codes
that telegraph: His cock. Stop. Their mouths. Stop.

He hands them their limp shorts, then dresses them
with his eyes, palm flat on their sunken chests
says, "Your heart chakra," then gives them his best

smile—great, wide, broad enough to swallow Jonah
boats, and harbors in its deep whale of rancor.

13. even through storms

My new lover will not know me as a man
who used to have a head of abundant
shampooed, coiffed, nutmeg hair. He will not see
the man who bounded UP subway stairs steep

as diamond runs. He won't recall wistfully
my sleeping all night not needing to pee
even through storms. Won't mind reminding me
by text, email, and phone that I'd promised—

does it matter much what it may have been?
He will not know my parents, what I wished
I'd done before I turned forty or sixty
and never known the drunk I was, how pissed.

The wishing wells are full of many coins.
I'll toss one more in. I'll pull it from my groin.

14. an ode to extra-corporeal membrane oxygenation and onychomycosis & an almost elegy

after 11 days at the cardiac care unit at beth israel deaconess medical center, boston, ma

"How beautiful are the feet." —Romans, 10:15

i.

His heart stopped—not like it does
before the silent fox or caribou
stopped—not like once
when *you* meant you.

ii.

They found his heart
had never ceased—his heart
a dog, too tired for sleep
had slept again, soundly.

iii.

God came down his throat.
When He pulled out
he hardly spoke—
how heaven intubates!

iv.

What comfort lies in rectangles
when he craves halos, circles
Vitruvian man, the Eucharist's
host, paper-thin, chaste, tasteless?

v.

Here's the Trinity:
ventilators, catheters, johnnies
looking straight in his eye
not untrue, not unkind.

vi.

He discovered on his feet
two black dots, bones
unriven still, places nails are driven
dark butcher marks for cleaving.

vii.

Ingrid, the nurse from Guatemala
explained, Sharpie—places
surgeons measure distances.
She washed his feet with Purell.

viii.

The unwatched soul hovers
on untethered wings, whole
and in night's magic circle
lives deeply, a thousand-fold.

ix.

Enmeshed in a bowerbird's nest
tangle of wires, tubes, IV's
pressure cuffs, heartbeats bleating
he stretches his eyes his body's length.

x.

He inspected his still useless feet—
right toenails, lovely crescents
pink of health, the left
sage grouse claws, yellow green.

xi.

He could walk circles all day
could open his mouth, put on socks
paint his fetid cuticles or sob.
It's toe fungus. For fuck's sake.

xii.

Was your shit a spiral or a loaf?
Your piss Red Sea or clear bone broth?
God asked. *That traffic light where you fell*
remember, those three perfect circles?

xiii.

Light was green, God said, *Go.*
Yellow, God said, *Pause.*
When it turned red at Summit Ave.
God said, *Stop*, and sent the ambulance.

xiv.

Busy doctors ignore him, Ah!
Say, *Ah!* (alpha) *Open your eyes!* (omega).
Between them, the gulf of the alphabet.
Not a man to bet, he waits.

Then I'm finally awake.

15. rare to medium-rare

Duffy is dying. He's handsome as ever.
When he tells me this, I'm mid-spoon in lobster

bisque at a five-star joint called Artisans
here in Houston where he has come again

to be retold the news that he's not worse
but not better either. It is the first

time I have seen him in four or five years.
I reach out for his last hand. I can hear

my heartbeat in the incomprehensible
boner that grows electric when he tells

me *I* was the one he'd leave his wife for.
He'd choose the funeral music. The words—

"tasteful," though—would be mine. "Geez, what a place!
Best damned steak, I have ever had," he says.

16. secret

"nunc et in hora mortis nostrae"
—Ave Maria

Give it to me in the full blast of sun.
Take it from me when the grasshopper hops.
Keep it with you on crushed oyster shell paths
through the spikes of lavender, with the breaths
of starlings releasing their very top
notes, the sweat of all the poppies, spun

with the ruby of their petals. Can you?
Will you? Some things we ask are difficult.
Some impossible and some vital, too:
vulcanized tears, laughter, guilt, anger's pulse.

Tell it to my mother in the last mist
of life. Whisper it to my father's grave.
But, please, keep it secret from me. Just kiss
me now and at the hour we're not brave.

17. on the "s" line

Fall in love every day a thousand times
at least. With that morning when the crossandras

bloom in a hue that seems new, that reminds
you of the lust immanent in oranges

with the buzzing of the least of the flies
which sound today unlike they have before.

Gaze, as if for the first time, at your eyes
falling into their waters, amazed more

than ever by this genetic trick, this
miracle. Touch gently a dying leaf.

Sense in it the virility of its
youth (*yours*). Fall in love with the small, the brief:

The passenger on the subway who smiles
not at you but love him that little while.

18. it is still still *(early onset alzheimer's)*

At high noon, the cardinal king presided
over the autumn olive (four long months

from blooming swoons into the fall) and lighted
the bush with a red like Lucifer Mont-

Bretia that itself would not reveal its
spikes and shatter the garden bed with music

of its particular blossoms that fit
a handshake (barely), at the cusp of thick

July heat, before August's moons, until
monardas and phlox had begun to take

sway over the whole bed. It is still still.
I sense his breath, though he's yards away, saving

the hours, looking out the frosted window
vacantly, not knowing yet what I know.

19. un mardi en septembre 2001, temps ordinaire—
a tuesday in september 2001, ordinary time

Prenons, par exemple, le beau signe
d'un cygne, qui est une seule ligne

Consider, for instance, the lovely sign
of a swan, which is but a single line

faite par une seule plume sur l'eau du lac :
la trace de Zeus après l'attaque.

that's made by one feather upon the lake:
a trail Zeus left after Leda's rape.

On dit : L'habit ne fait pas le moine.
Le dieu trompeur pèche sans témoignes

They say, don't judge a book by its cover.
The deceitful god sins without a witness

quand le soleil se couche ou les feuilles
le cachent aux yeux mortels. Que tu veuilles

when leaves obscure him or when the sun sets
away from mortal eyes. That you should hover

attendre avec moi—une belle
chose ! Il y en a tant qui se mêle

here with me, waiting—a beautiful thing!
There are so many lovely things that mingle

avec les choses qui sont affreuses :
le matin où nous nous sommes rencontrés

with the horrid ones: that morning with
our eyes landing on each other with this:

les avions—flèches dans la clarté—
nous coupa le souffle, coupa nombreuse.

those planes—arrows shooting through limpid space—
took our breath—and countless others'—away.

20. trachelospermum jasminoides

A night of firsts this last of February:
the new smells of fuggish air my first year

in Texas, where trellised jessamine steals
my breath, south of the Mason-Dixon, where

the flower's own taxonomy, Jasminium
is trumped by the common name used here: creeping

confederate jasmine. How, when will we
reconcile names with truths, which rub some

folk the wrong way, but rub too many out?
There must be banalities in memories

gasps of joy, and some severities that
can't be shaken from shoulders, washed from hands.

Take now the breath of that seductress jasmine.
Farsi for "gift *from* God," Not yours. Not mine.

21. catatumbo

The terminus of it all can be
an empty station or a beehive.
Bees expire; honey never spoils.

(¿Qué te dijo, mijo, cuando se fue?
¿Que se iba a vagar por el mar?
¿A cuál mar, mi amor, a cúal?)

Anger is fear turned inside
out, like mango skins inverted
to reveal the fruits' pulp.

(¿Te quiere mucho, mi criatura?
Cuando te agarra por la cintura
¿te corta el aliento, te para el corazón?)

From the Cota Mil's foot path
walk to the top, feel the blue gasp
of ocean on the Ávila's other side.

(Si van temprano el aire del monte
será dulce como almbimar, fresco
y verde como líquido vidrio de mar.)

This you wish he'd know of you
Catatumbo's House of Thunder
its river's mirror-cracking lightning.

(Madre, si tan sólo supiera cómo
salvar este buque que yo naufragé
y encontrar el sueño que huyó de mi.)

Patience is alabaster, kitten milk
because when he fucks you outside
your lather will baptize you both.

(Sé que algun día se abrirará tu pecho
como un abanico, perderás el temor
del agua y te bañarás en su luz.)

Seeing you nude, the moon will wink.

22. dispatches from amnesty international

reuters: caracas, venezuela, november, 14, 2025: trump
officials hold meetings on venezuela as military tensions rise

The last racemes of banana trees
dogs, barking, sarcophagi-bellied
the firecracker japes, the riddles
of bullets through cinderblocks.

(Who would winnow in the first
tree, laughing tree, laughing last
note by note, the black puma
brow singed with recklessness?)

In Miraflores Palace, Putin's crude
black caviar, Erdogan's boats
of dates, Jinping's unlimited
data plans and above Maduro's bed

(Would I, patient as alabaster,
curry, cosset, cringe, retreating
prows, shattering rivers of tannins
so red they wait for me to flame?)

in la Casona, Chiquinquirá
our virgin besieged, embarrassed
by nards, gardenias, orchids, musks
smog, the radiant putrid flesh

(What morrow, distant as poles
mingles with me now that weeps
the razor's edge sucked clean
brings me to my knees?)

while shards of fishermen boats spike
the air, like flying fish fins bursting
from international waters that know
no laws since all's fair game.

(Where keen mountains
tumbling into shore, aflame
paper boats doves taking flight
burning into ozone, dead?)

You save if you lose, and we're lost.

23. piss poor

> *"Those who have never suffered the iniquities of exile cannot possibly understand the significance, the gravitas, of a mattress."*
> *—Ariel Dorfman*

Home? Where's home? Twenty-seven years of exile
each one lived single file, hawks circling ever
closer, ever lower, never alighting
enough to feed on the crumbs of whatever

remained of us, although we always hungered
worse than raptors, reeked rank like carrion, stirred
grimier dirt than combines, thirsted far
more than New York City marathoners

who've never had to sprint to stay alive
never crossed tombs or hurdled over borders
through Andes' brumes to reach the other side
never thought, *Where's home?* and arriving at

the finish line, were swiftly wrapped in mylar blankets
while we asked, *Where's home?*, pissed in cups, then drank it.

24. the birds that live at the home depot

The birds that live at Home Depot don't care
if you find someone in a yellow apron

to help you find screws or bolts that you dared
unscrew, knowing full-well you are a moron

with hardware and even one damned lightbulb.
They swoop. They poop. They twitter. They lie waiting

for sprouting fruit trees, bareroot roses, bulbs
the bags of birdseed you've torn open, late

for closing hour at the Jack in the Box
around the corner. They tweet. Swoop. They know

by your harried gait which of you just stocked
up on Snickers for fifty tomorrows.

The birds that live at Lowe's don't care much either
who screws, gets screwed. They swoop. They poop. They twitter.

notes

2. thirteen (fourteen) ways of looking at the faggot

I am riffing on the poem by Wallace Stevens (1879–1955) "Thirteen Ways of Looking at the Blackbird."

I am alluding to the poem "Talking in Bed" by Philip Larkin (1922–1985): "It becomes still more difficult to find/Words at once true and kind,/Or not untrue and not unkind."

10. en el autobus (on the city bus)

My English translations for my texts in Spanish are as follows: second stanza, "I repair to the bedroom/where my childhood feet/unstockinged, remained./What might it be like to expire/in this very same bed/where I was birthed?"; fourth stanza, "When time wakes up/in its own good time—/like you—it stays silent./See how the stairsteps quietly rise on their own,/weary. of our ascents and descents"; and sixth stanza, "The hours we steal from ourselves,/the ledgers we keep that count us/the desires that die in the soul/loves that flee from us/all live on dead-end streets."

13. an ode to extra-corporeal membrane oxygenation and onychomycosis & an almost elegy

An Extra-Corporeal Membrane Oxygenation machine is a last-ditch life-support apparatus.

Onychomycosis is the medical term for toe fungus.

Section vi. is my own translation of the final stanza of the poem by Hermann Hesse (1877–1962) "Beim Schlafengehen," famously one of the texts used by Richard Strauss (1864–1949) for his 1948 valedictory song cycle, *Vier Letzte Lieder* (Four Last Songs): *"Und die Seele unbewacht/will in freien Flügen schweben/Um im Zauberkreis der Nacht/Tief und tausendfach zu leben."*

16. secret

The epigraph of this poem is the final line of the Hail Mary prayer: "Now and in the hour of our death."

17. on the "s" line

The "s" line of New York City's Metropolitan Transit Authority is a shuttle that runs between Grand Central Station–42nd Street and Times Square–42nd Street. It is the city's shortest subway line.

21. catatumbo
The Cota Mil (in English, "Elevation One Thousand") in Caracas, Venezuela, also known as Avenida Boyacá, with an elevation of one thousand meters, is a highway found in the capital city's northern sector, at the foot of the Ávila National Park, which is located in the Cordillera de la Costa (Coastal Mountain Range) and separates the valley where Caracas sits from the country's Caribbean coast.

On the Catatumbo River in western Venezuela, on as many as 140 nights every year, for nine hours at a time, lightning strikes at a rate of between sixteen and forty times a minute, a rare phenomenon arising from a mass of storm clouds hovering higher than one kilometer. Catatumbo has the world's highest incidence and concentration of lightning.

My own translations for my texts in Spanish in this poem are as follows: second stanza, "What did he tell you, my son, when he left?/That he was going to wander the seas?/Which sea, my love, which?"; fourth stanza, "Does he love you very much, my baby?/When he grabs you by the waist/ does he take your breath away, break your heart?"; sixth stanza, "If you go early the mountain air/will be sweet as nectar, fresh/and green as liquid sea glass"; eighth stanza, "Mother, if I only knew how/to save this vessel I shipwrecked/and find the dream that fled from me"; and tenth stanza, "I know that one day your chest will open/like a fan, you'll lose your fear/of waters, will bathe in their light."

22. dispatches from amnesty international
Miraflores Palace in the capital city of Caracas is the Venezuelan equivalent of the US Capitol Building, and the Casona (the big house) is the presidential residence.

The Virgin of Chiquinquirá is the patroness saint of Zulia state in western Venezuela. I have imagined that Nicolás Maduro (b. 1962)—the former dictator of Venezuela who was removed from power by American military forces in January 2026 and imprisoned in the US to face charges of narco-terrorism and importing cocaine—had done the unthinkable, desecrating this holy relic by hanging it over his bed.

The interspersed text in italics depicts the abnegation and duress endured under Maduro's "socialism," which robbed people of basic daily necessities such as shelter, food, and water, and rendering words and thoughts virtually nonsensical—the grammar of everyday language, logic, and of life itself became fractured, having emerged out of loss, need, and deprivation.

23. piss poor
Since Venezuela's now dead President Hugo Chávez (1954–2013) established the Bolivarian Republic in 1999, there has been a mass emigration from my homeland, now numbering over 8.5 million (equal to nearly 22% of the country's population). Many who flee on foot through the Andes to neighboring Colombia are called "los caminantes," the walkers.

Born and raised in Venezuela of a Venezuelan mother and an American father and growing up speaking and writing in Spanish, English, and French, **Richard Haney-Jardine** came to the US at fifteen to study at Phillips Exeter Academy, where he had the extraordinary opportunity of working individually (albeit briefly) with Pulitzer Prize-winning Gwendolyn Brooks, Jorge Luis Borges, one of the most venerated voices in Latin American literature, and Thom Gunn, a queer poet who opened the door to Richard's exploration of his sexuality. Until today, in the school's 240-year history, he is the only sophomore to have received Exeter's distinguished Lewis Sibley Poetry Award, and he still holds the record of winning this award more than once, garnering this accolade in three consecutive years. As a young writer of eighteen, he received awards from *The Boston Globe*, which published his work, and five awards from *Scholastic Magazine*, which named him Artist of the Year in 1982, inviting him to present a reading on the stage of Carnegie Hall.

He received a full scholarship to Harvard, from which he was graduated in 1985, having studied with the Mexican polymath Carlos Fuentes, Helen Vendler, one of the premiere scholars and critics of poetry in English, and, for three years, with Nobel Laureate Seamus Heaney as his one-on-one tutor. Subsequently, he was awarded a grant to the Sorbonne to pursue graduate work in the philosophy of the French Enlightenment. Over the next three decades, he held senior editorial positions at Houghton Mifflin Publishing Company, Sony Classical Recordings, and Carnegie Hall, as well as other important national and international classical music venues, where he translated scores of poems, libretti, and Lieder texts from and into several languages. In 2019, at age 55, he enrolled in Emerson College's MFA program, graduating in 2022, receiving several graduate awards, including two consecutive Academy of American Poets Awards, adding to the two he had received in college three decades earlier. At Emerson, he worked with the widely published poet Daniel Tobin, memoirist and poet Richard Hoffman, Pulitzer Winner Megan Marshall, and distinguished poet Christine Casson.

Sixty-two now, he is only in his second year of seeking professional publication. Already, his work has been published by *The Iowa Review*, the websites of The Academy of American Poets and Winning Writers, in the anthologies, *HABITS: The Good, The Bad, and The Ugly* and *One Page Poetry*, and he was won several notable prizes. This chapbook, printed by Finishing Line Press, is his first solo publication.

www.ingramcontent.com/pod-product-compliance
Lightning Source LLC
LaVergne TN
LVHW090539110826
845146LV00003B/1179

* 9 7 9 8 8 9 9 9 0 4 7 5 2 *